Written by©
Lindi Masters

Illustrated by©
Lizzie Masters

"GATEWAYS, DNA AND JACOB'S LADDER"
Copyright© 2019

Story written by Lindi Masters
Illustrated and Designed by Lizzie Masters

Thank you to IGNITE KIDZHUB© and all the kids that take part from around the world, for their artwork.
Special thanks to our mentors and friends Ian Clayton and Grant Mahoney, without whom we wouldn't have explored these realms.
Published by seraph Creative in 2019
seraphcreative.org
ISBN: 978-0-6486985-5-5

All rights reserved.© No part of this publication may be reproduced, stored in a retrieval system or transmitted, in any form or by any means, electronic, mechanical, photocopying, recording or otherwise, without the prior permission of the copyright holder.

All rights reserved.© No part of this book, artwork included may be used or reproduced in any manner without the written permission of the publisher.

This Book Belongs to:
_____

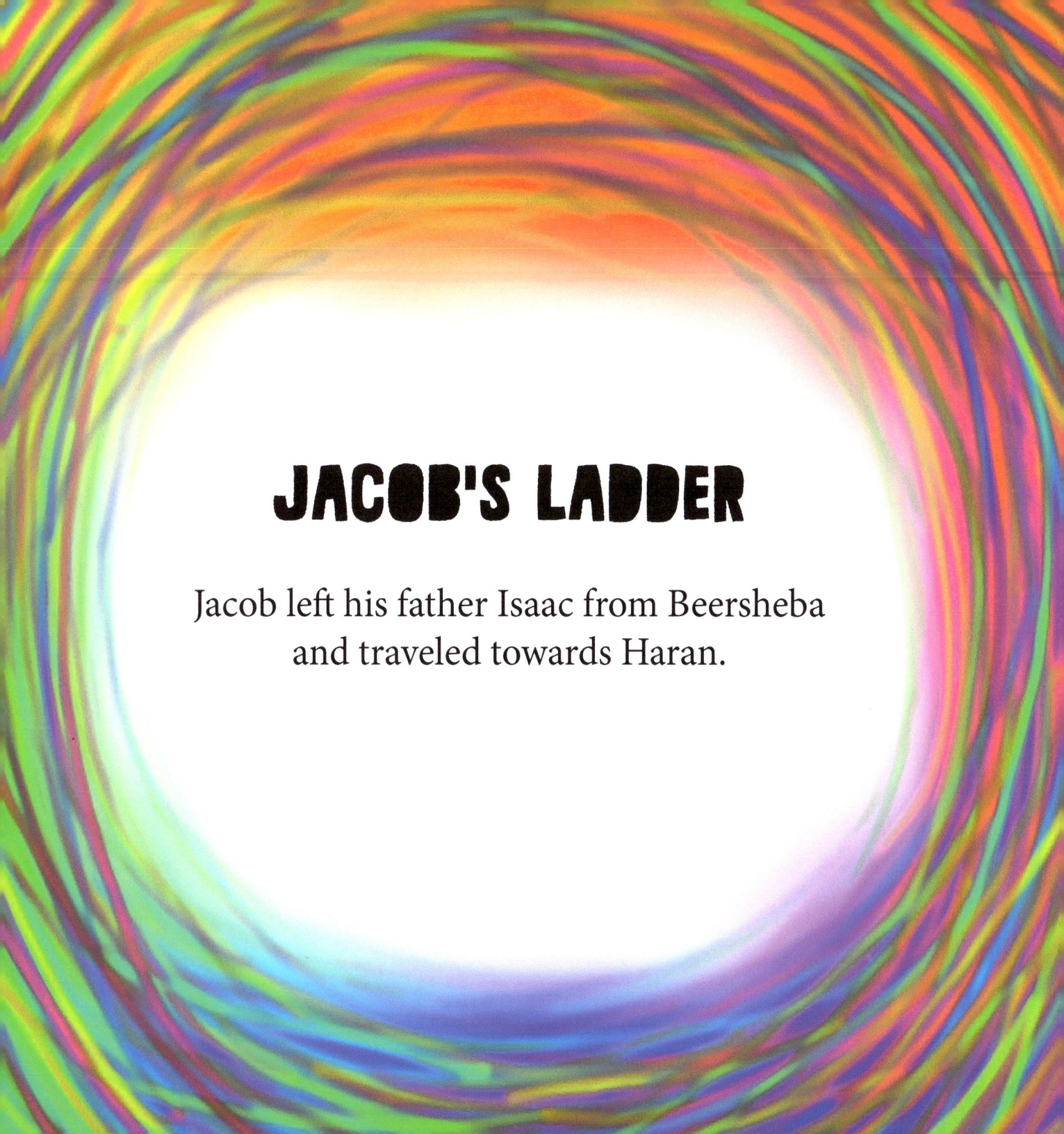

JACOB'S LADDER

Jacob left his father Isaac from Beersheba and traveled towards Haran.

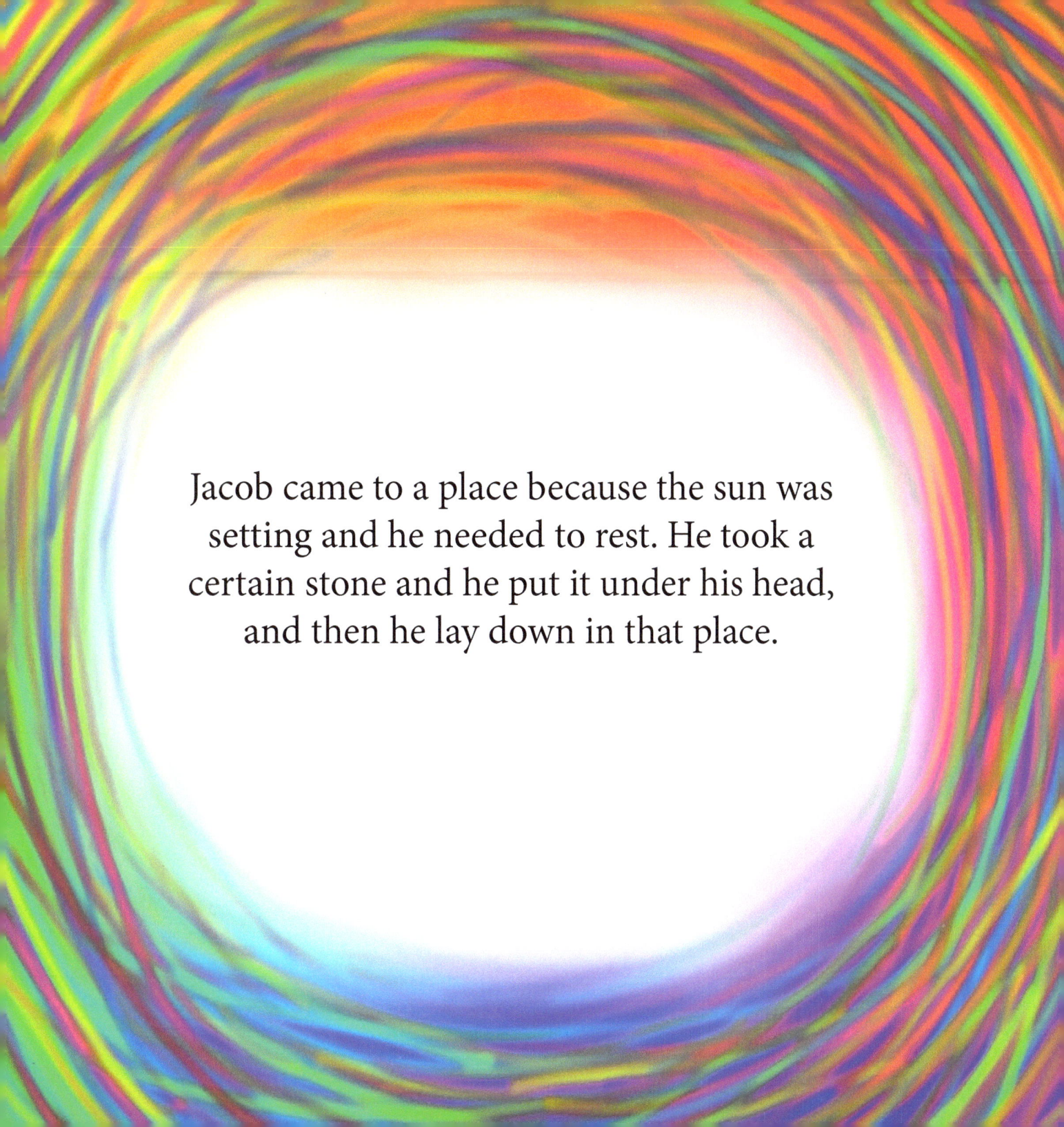

Jacob came to a place because the sun was setting and he needed to rest. He took a certain stone and he put it under his head, and then he lay down in that place.

Sometime after falling asleep, he dreamed and a ladder was setup on the earth coming from within him and its top reached up to Heaven. And there the Angels of Yahweh were ascending and descending on it.

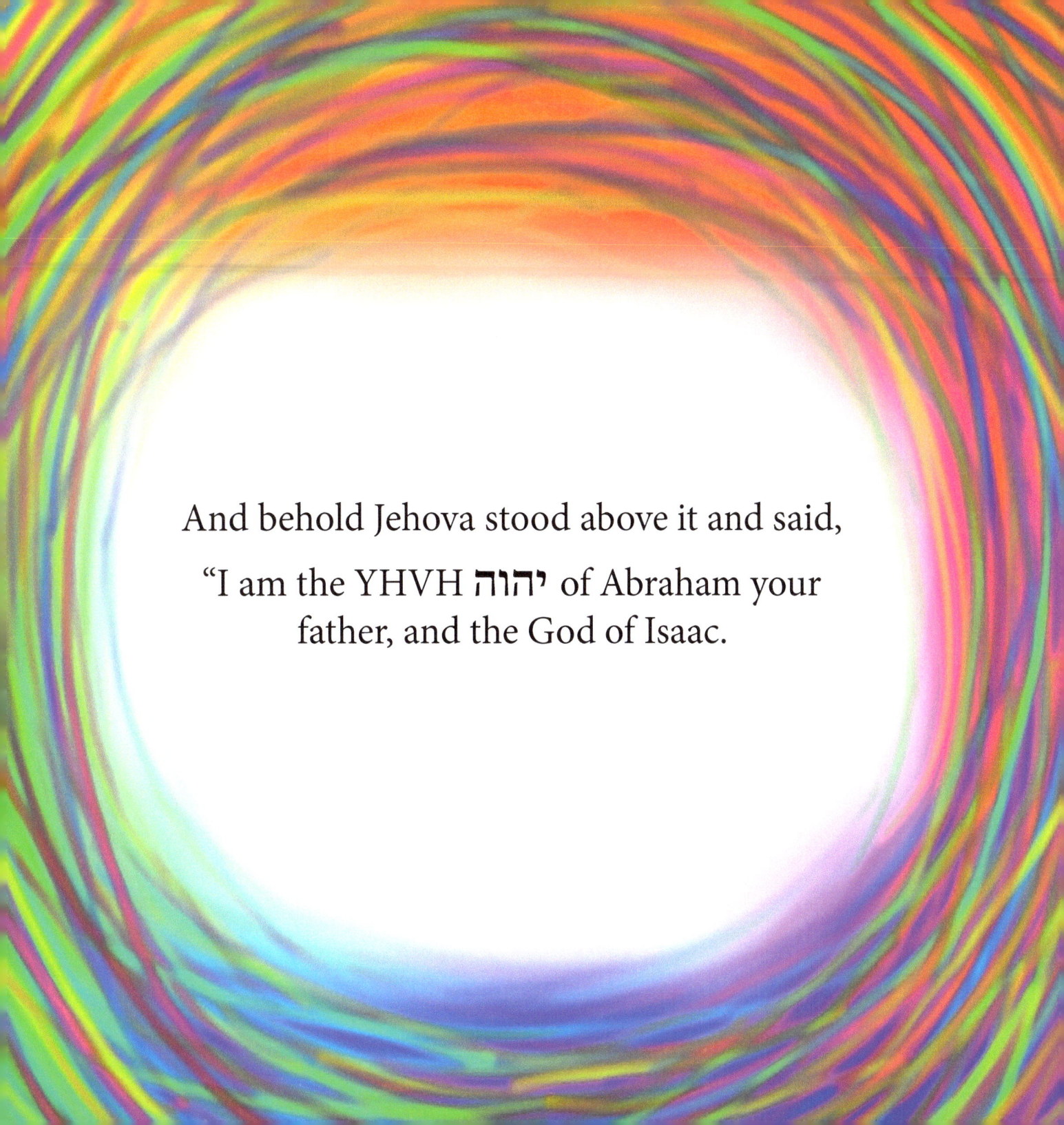

And behold Jehova stood above it and said,

"I am the YHVH יהוה of Abraham your father, and the God of Isaac.

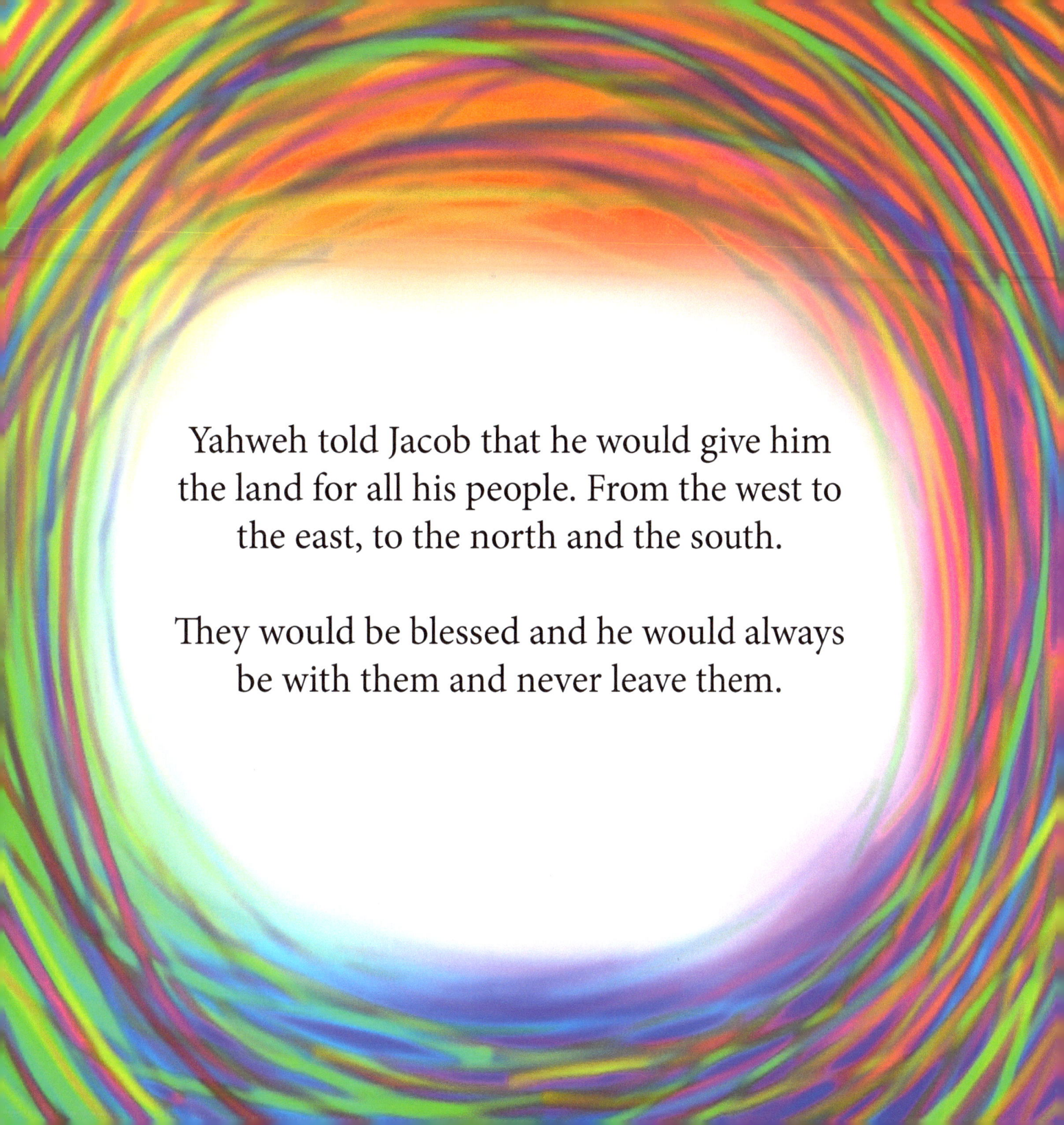

Yahweh told Jacob that he would give him the land for all his people. From the west to the east, to the north and the south.

They would be blessed and he would always be with them and never leave them.

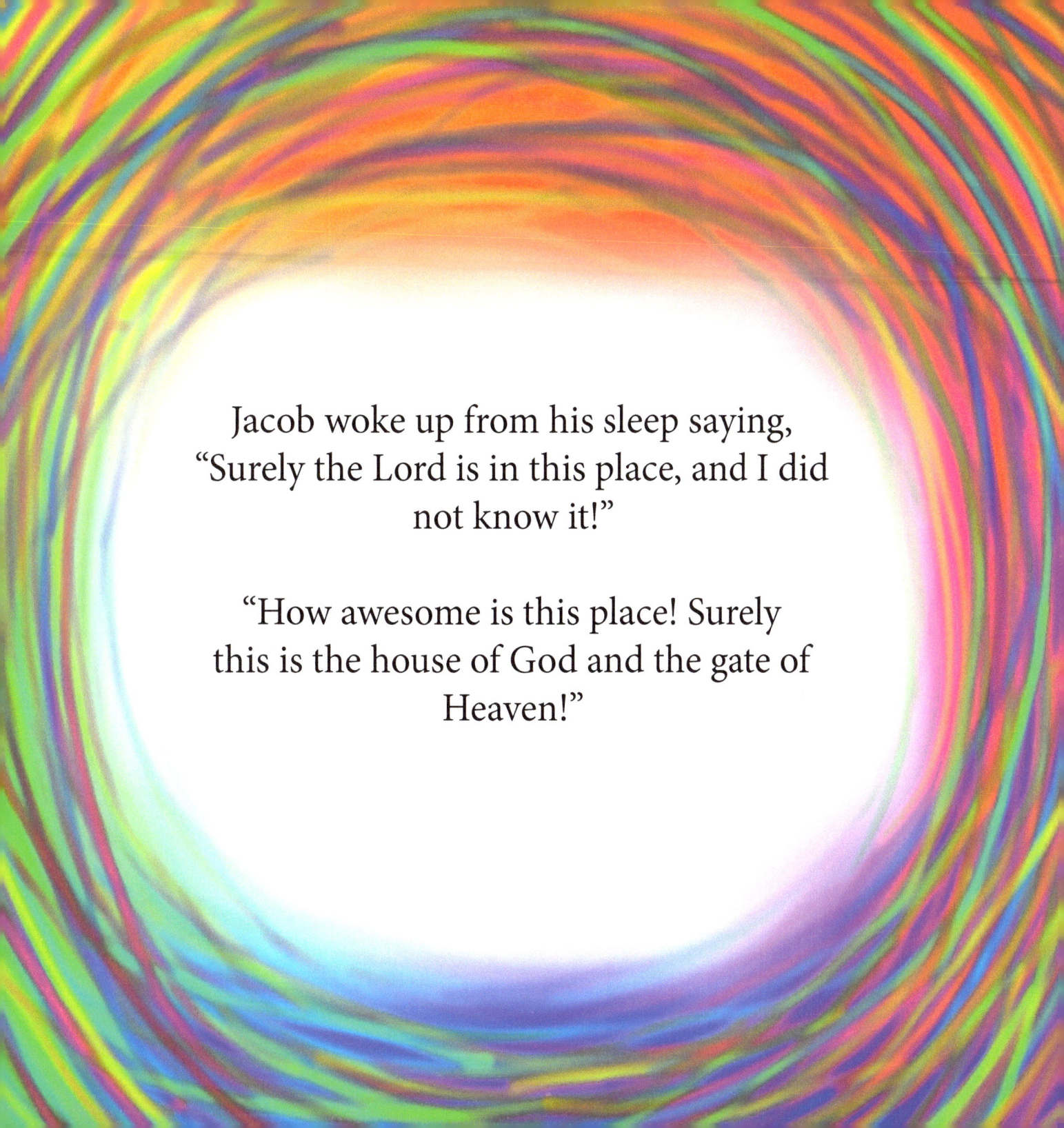

Jacob woke up from his sleep saying, "Surely the Lord is in this place, and I did not know it!"

"How awesome is this place! Surely this is the house of God and the gate of Heaven!"

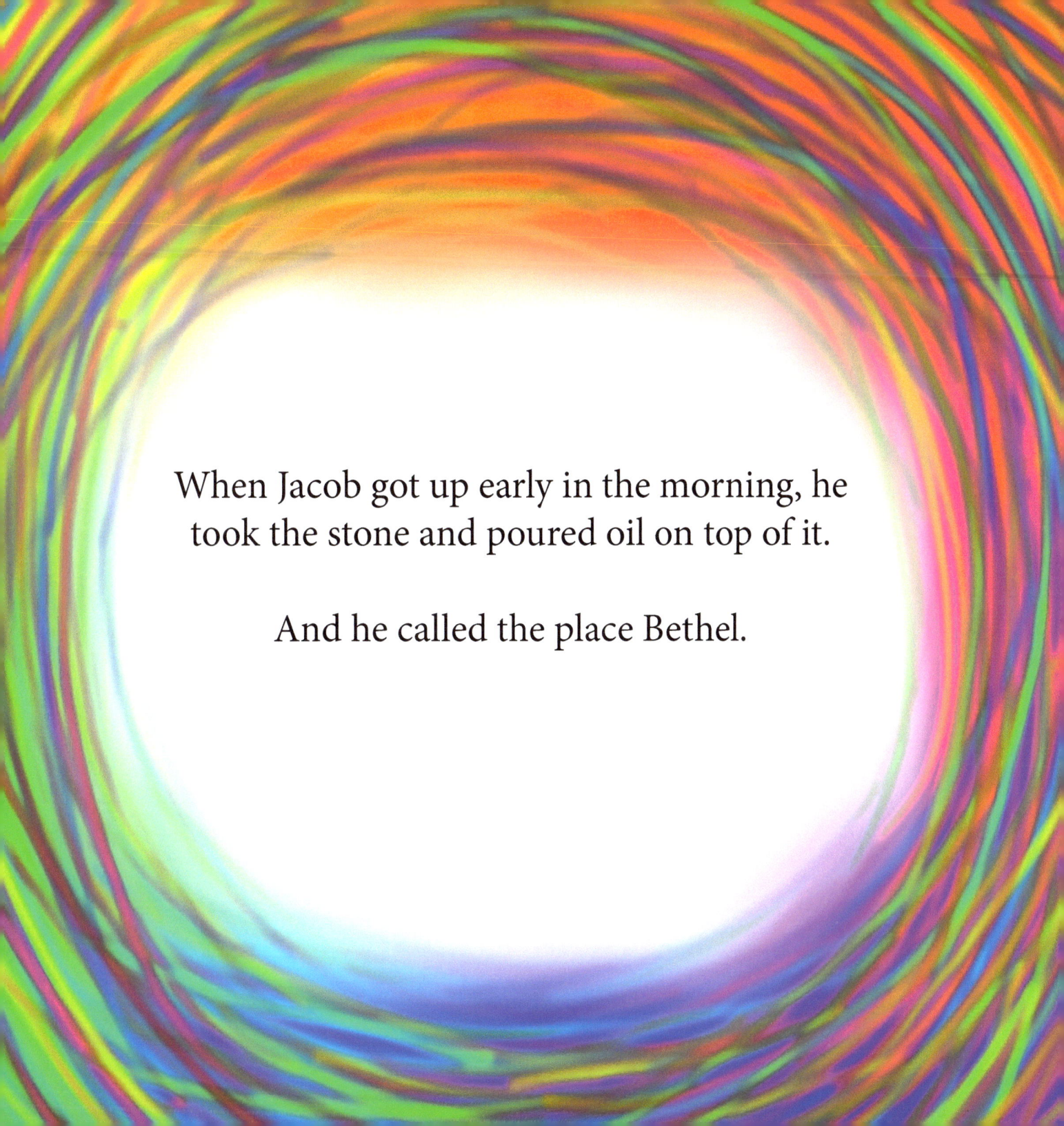

When Jacob got up early in the morning, he took the stone and poured oil on top of it.

And he called the place Bethel.

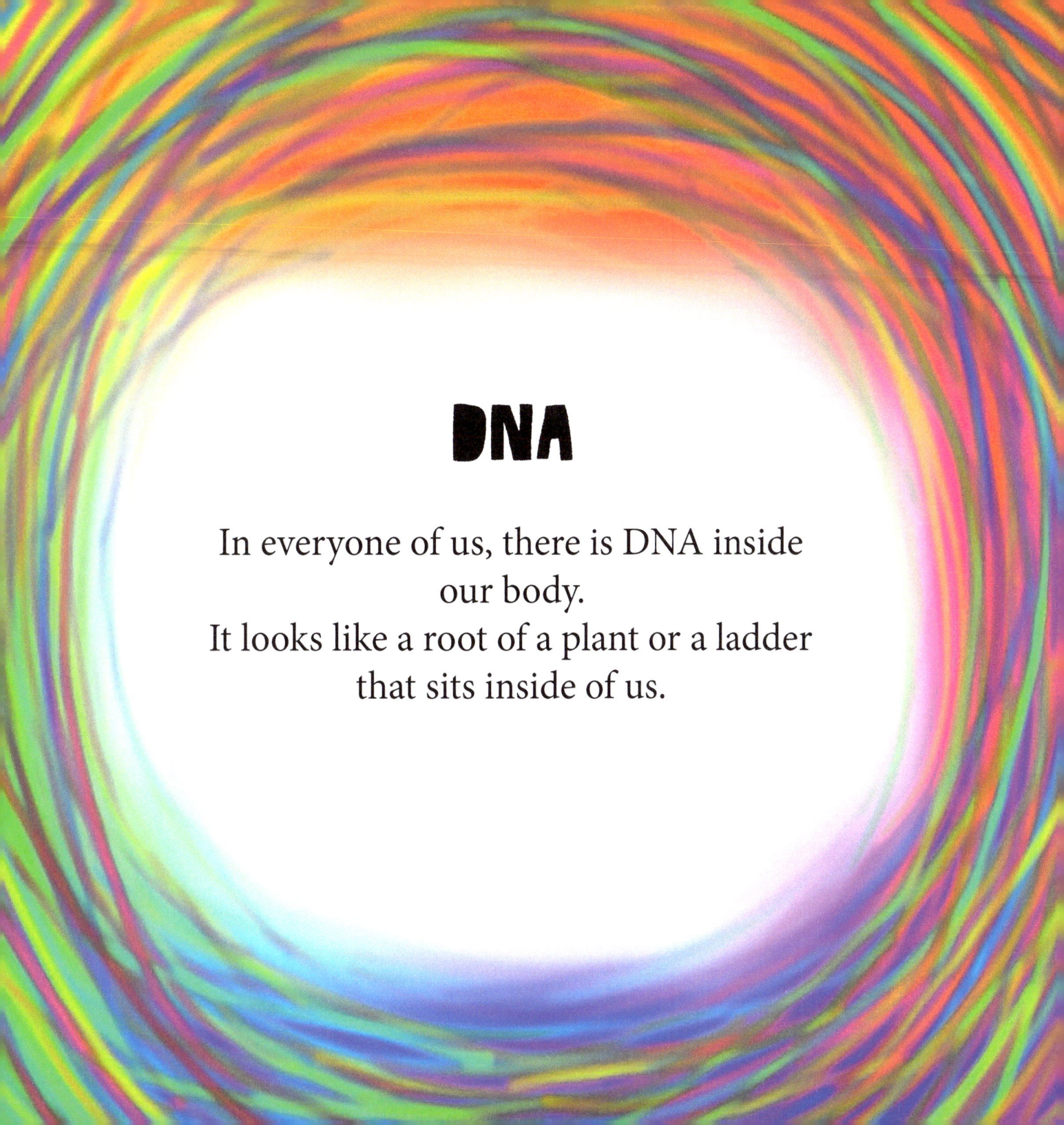

DNA

In everyone of us, there is DNA inside our body.
It looks like a root of a plant or a ladder that sits inside of us.

Our DNA carries the stories of our family and our ancestors.

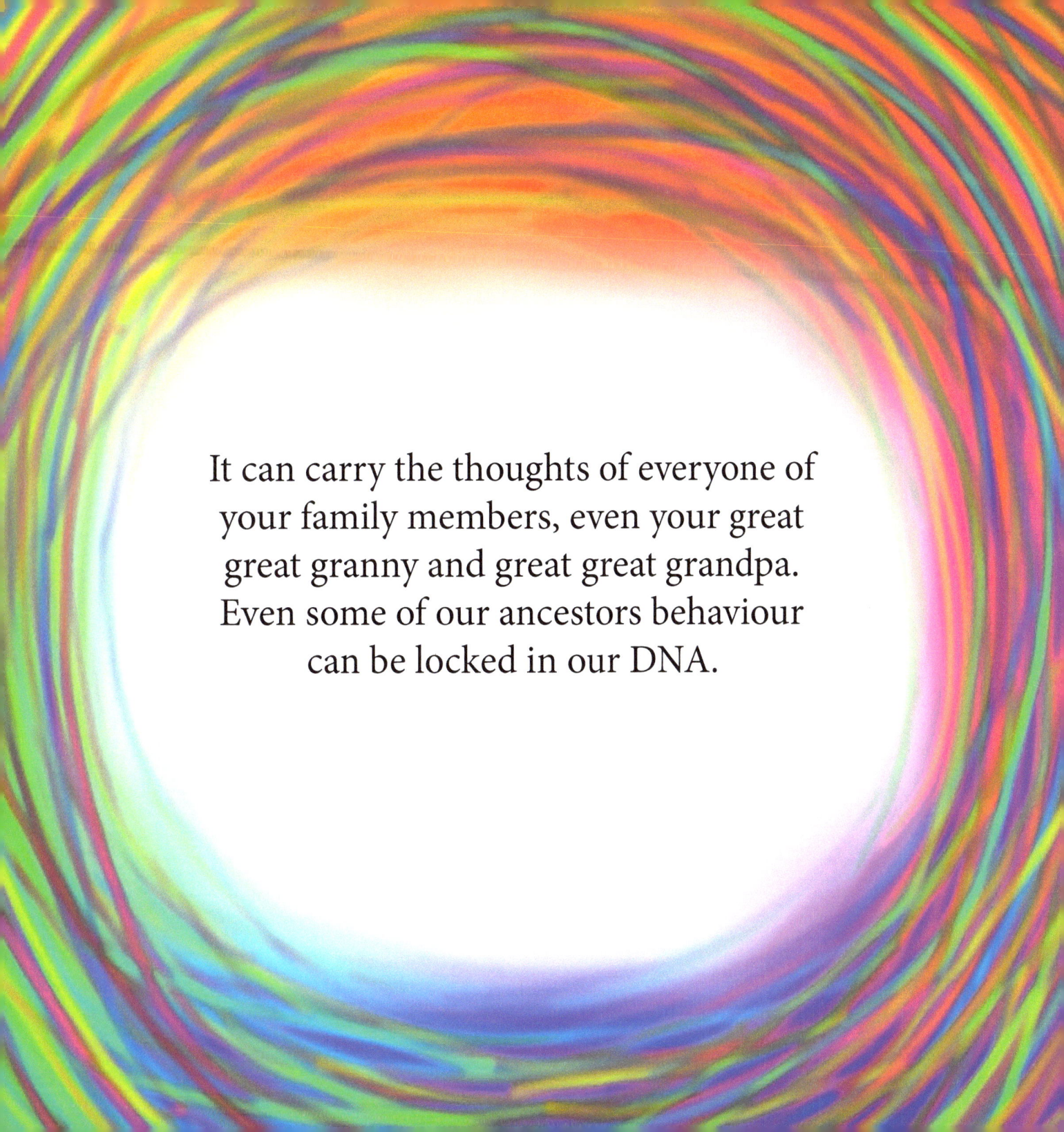

It can carry the thoughts of everyone of your family members, even your great great granny and great great grandpa. Even some of our ancestors behaviour can be locked in our DNA.

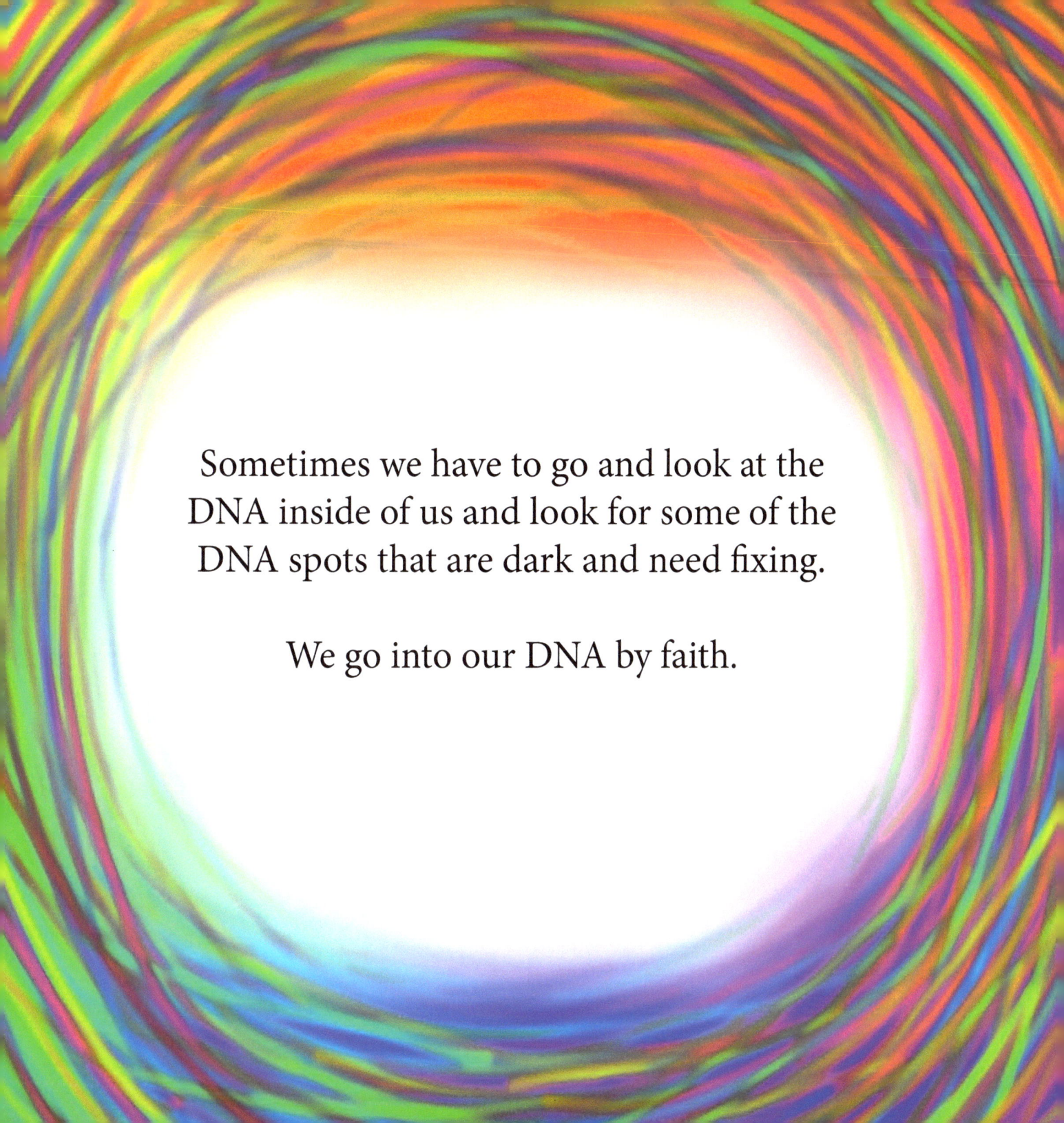

Sometimes we have to go and look at the DNA inside of us and look for some of the DNA spots that are dark and need fixing.

We go into our DNA by faith.

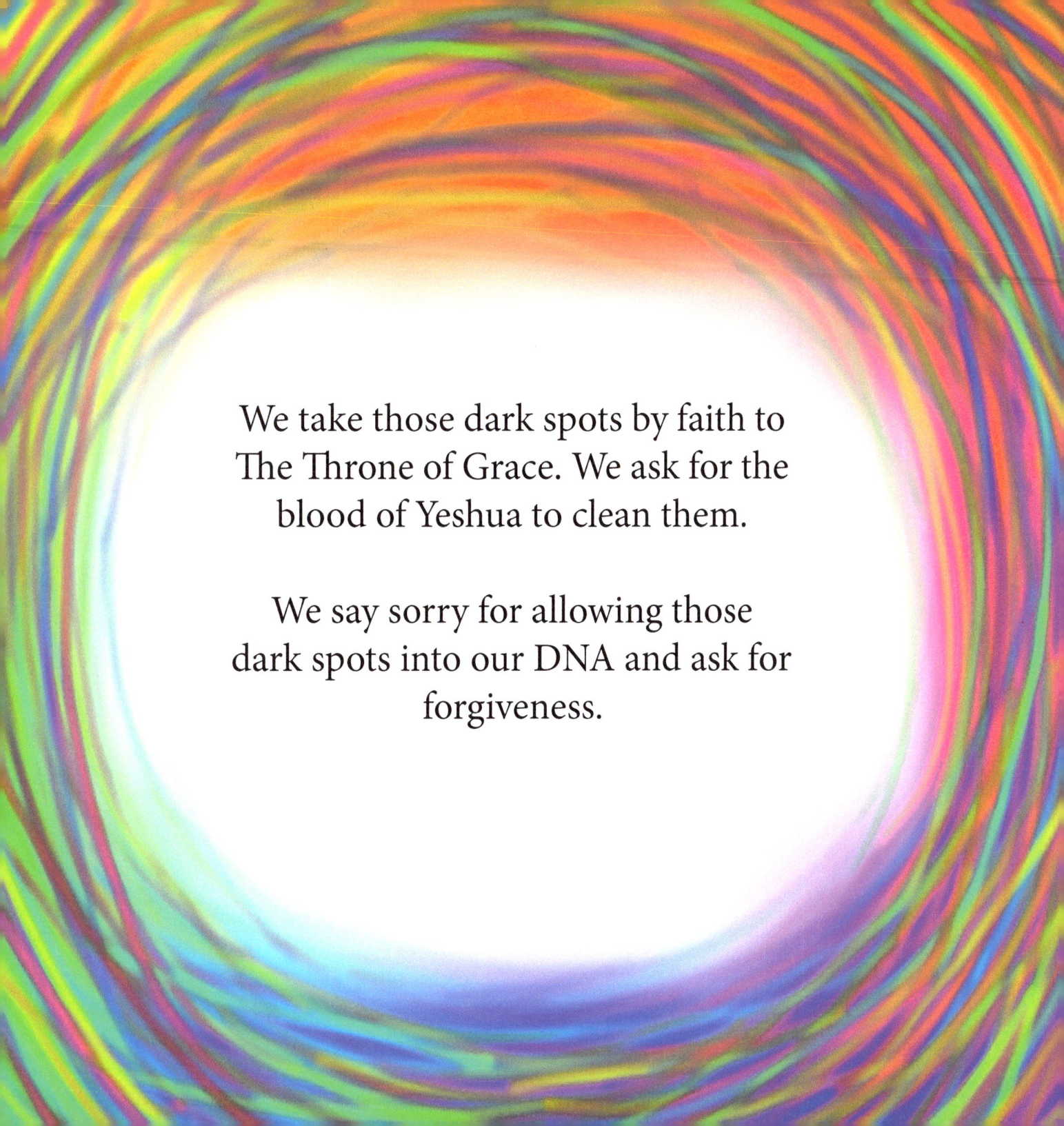

We take those dark spots by faith to The Throne of Grace. We ask for the blood of Yeshua to clean them.

We say sorry for allowing those dark spots into our DNA and ask for forgiveness.

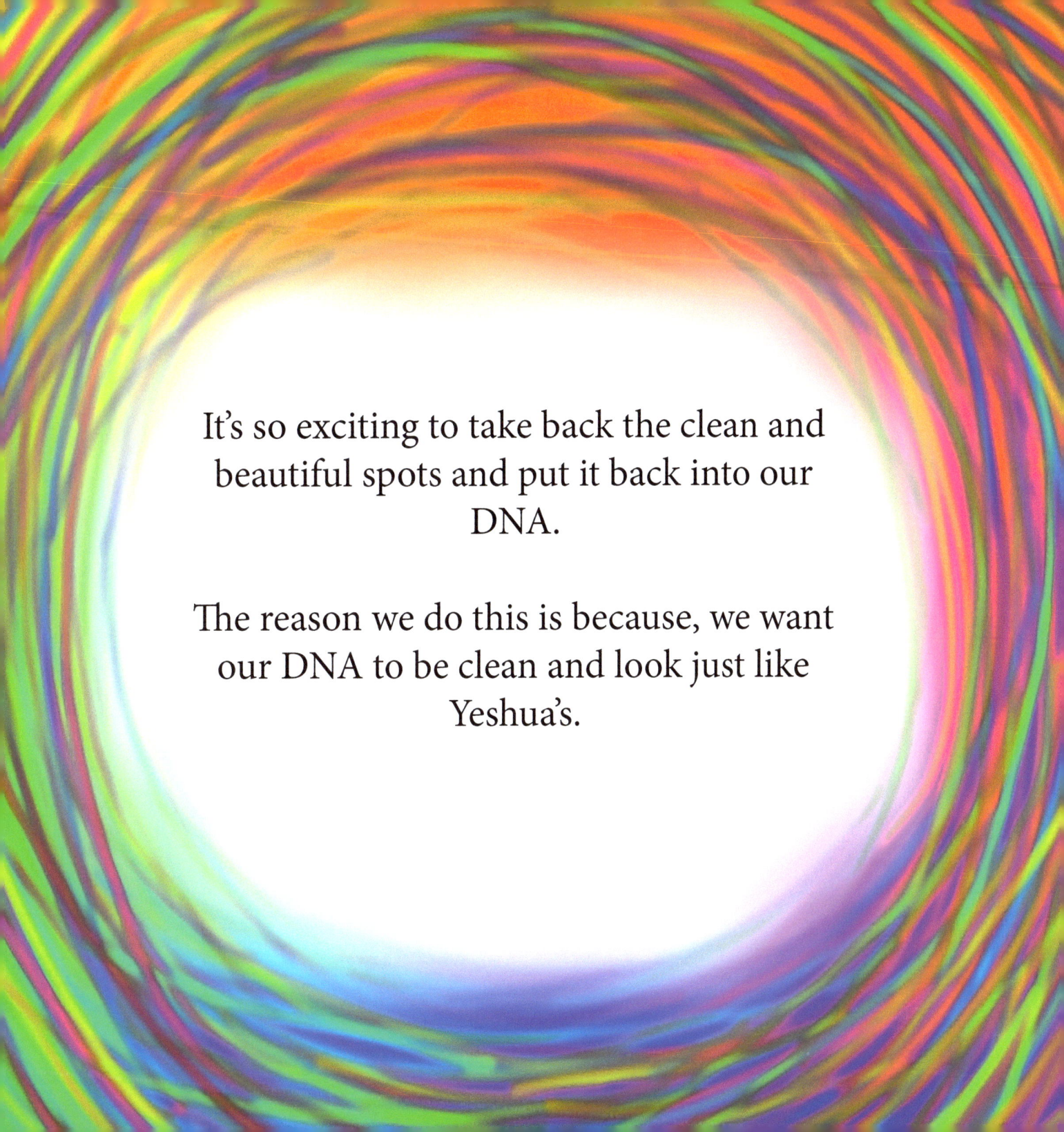

It's so exciting to take back the clean and beautiful spots and put it back into our DNA.

The reason we do this is because, we want our DNA to be clean and look just like Yeshua's.

GATEWAYS TO THE SPIRIT, SOUL AND BODY

Everyone of us has a spirit, soul and body. We have different gates in each one of them. Sometimes ha-satan comes and shuts those gates so that we can't see properly into Zion, where we come from.

We have been given The Word, The Sword of the Spirit, the Blood of Yeshua and His name יהוה. These help to open the gates.

Gateways of The Spirit

Yahweh I ask for forgiveness for letting chains cover my door of First Love. I speak יהוה into that door to open up my heart, Yahweh.

Thank you that the door of First Love to You is open.

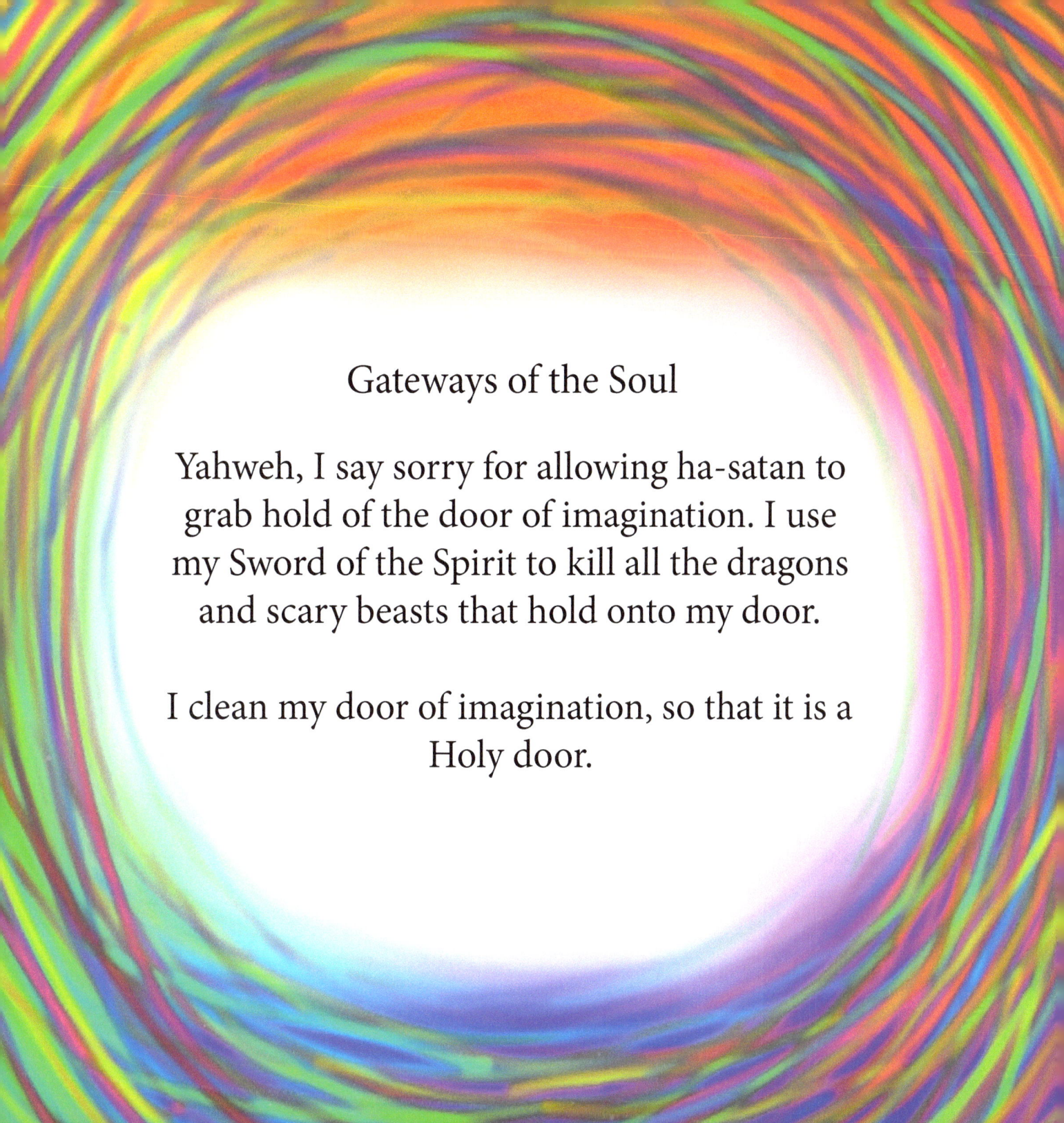

Gateways of the Soul

Yahweh, I say sorry for allowing ha-satan to grab hold of the door of imagination. I use my Sword of the Spirit to kill all the dragons and scary beasts that hold onto my door.

I clean my door of imagination, so that it is a Holy door.

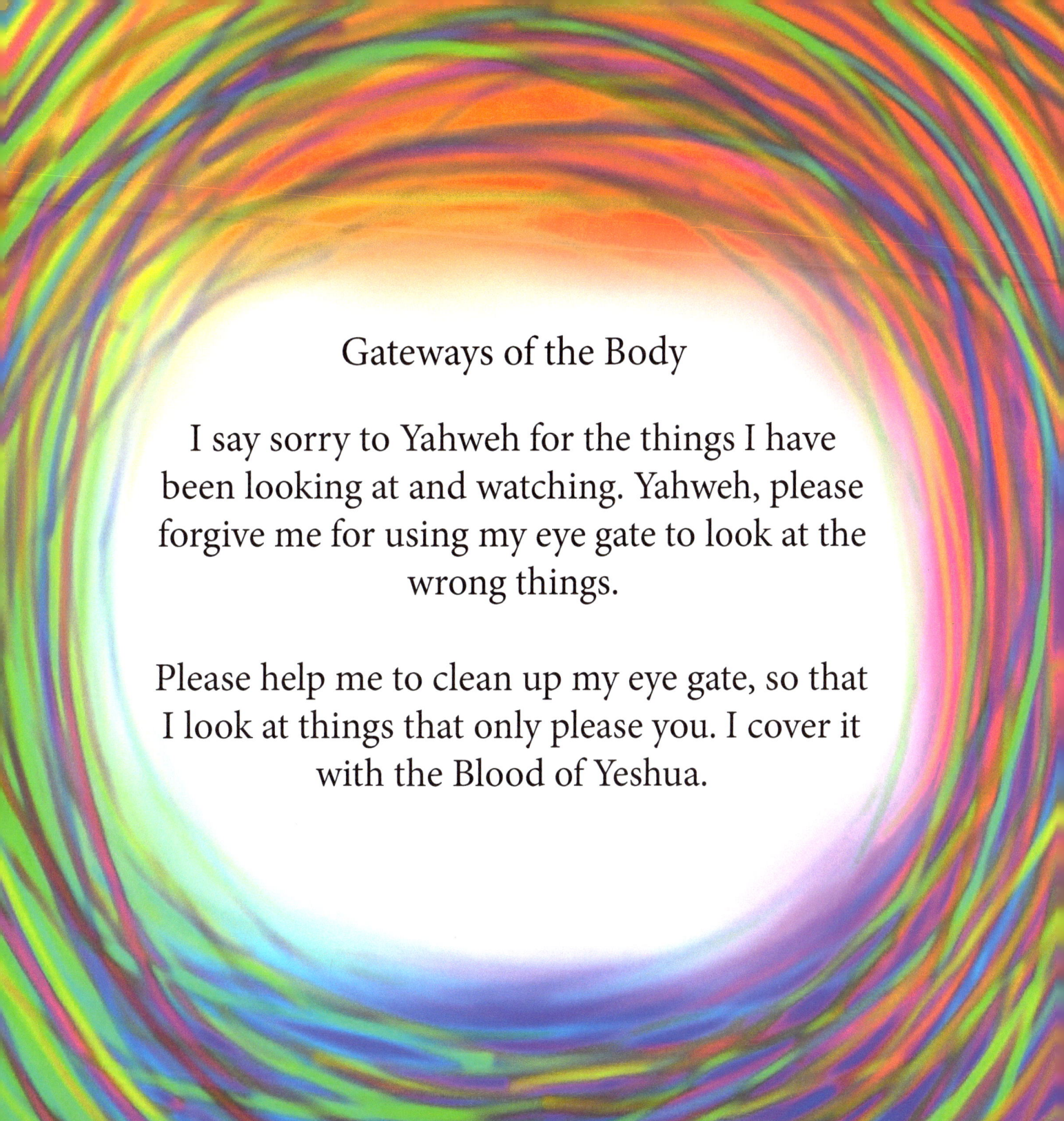

Gateways of the Body

I say sorry to Yahweh for the things I have been looking at and watching. Yahweh, please forgive me for using my eye gate to look at the wrong things.

Please help me to clean up my eye gate, so that I look at things that only please you. I cover it with the Blood of Yeshua.

Carla- Australia

Hannah- South Africa

Jeiel- UK

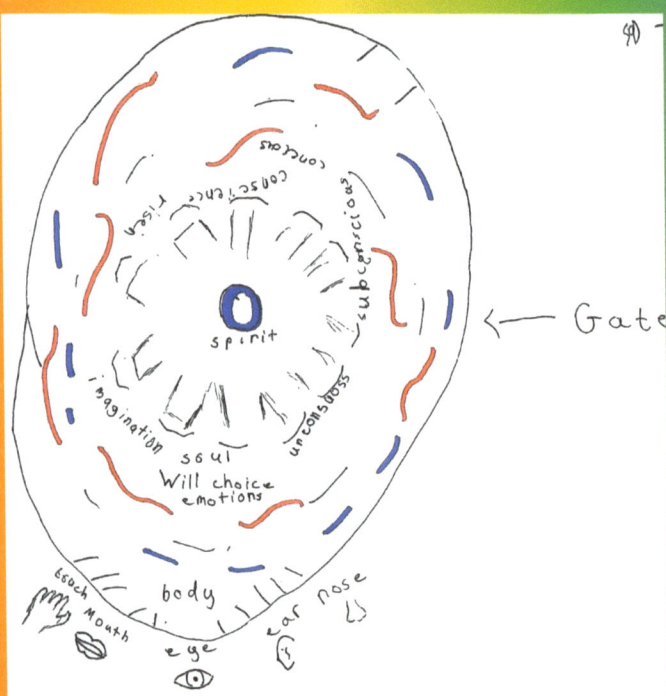

Levi- South Africa

Reuben- UK

Luke- Australia

Zoë- South Africa

Naomi- Australia

Reuben- UK

Jeiel- UK

Carla- Australia

Reuel- UK